ALL YOU NEED TO KNOW ABOUT...

Safari Animals

Contents

Life in the savannah — 6
The elephant is the biggest — 8
All about skin and trunks — 10
A family of girls — 12
The giraffe is the tallest — 14
Alone and in groups — 16
The zebra — 18
The rhinoceros — 20
Two horns – one big, one small — 22
The hippopotamus — 24
Hippos big and small — 26
The lion — 28
A king's life — 30
The cheetah — 32
A big hunter — 34
Records — 36
Index — 38

First published in Great Britain by
Cherrytree Books, part of the Evans Publishing Group
2A Portman Mansions
Chiltern Street
London W1U 6NR

Copyright © this edition Evans Brothers Limited 2004

Originally published under the title
'Mes Petites Encyclopédies Larousse Les dinosaures'
Copyright © LAROUSSE/VUEF 2002
Copyright © LAROUSSE/S.E.J.E.R 2004

Text by Agnès Vandewiele, Michèle Lancina

ISBN 1 84234 237 1

A CIP catalogue record for this book is available from the British Library

Printed in France

ALL YOU NEED TO KNOW ABOUT...

Safari Animals

Illustrated by **Jérôme Ruillier**

CHERRYTREE BOOKS

Life in the savannah

Many animals live in the open grasslands of Africa, called the savannah. It is very hot, but there is plenty of food for the animals to eat.

People like to
go on safari to
watch the animals
of the savannah.

7

The **elephant** is the biggest

An elephant weighs as much as a hundred people!

It is as big as a house.

It can live for up to eighty years. A male elephant keeps growing throughout his life.

It needs a lot to drink.

An elephant eats day and night and munches huge amounts of grass and leaves every day.

9

All about skin and trunks

An elephant's skin is thick but very sensitive.

Elephants are often bitten by insects,
but small birds help by feeding on the insects.

Elephants use their trunk to breathe underwater...

...to reach leaves from high branches

A useful trunk

...to shower

...to pull down trees

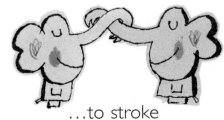

...to stroke
other elephants ... and to bellow!

11

A family of girls

Elephants live in herds of females from the same family: a mother and her daughters, with their own children. The oldest elephant is the leader. Male elephants usually live alone.

After birth, a baby elephant suckles its mother.

Young elephants love to play.

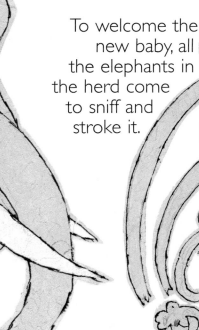

To welcome the new baby, all the elephants in the herd come to sniff and stroke it.

They also need a lot of rest: they go to sleep as soon as the herd stops moving.

13

The giraffe is the tallest

Thanks to its long neck and large tongue, a giraffe can reach the tender leaves right at the top of the trees.

Its favourite food is the acacia tree, which has lots of thorns.

A giraffe takes long strides when it walks, lifting up first its two left legs together, then its two right legs. Its long neck helps it to balance.

Giraffes are so tall that it is difficult for them to lie down. So they sleep standing up.

It's not easy for a giraffe to drink! Fortunately, it does not need a lot of water.

Male giraffes use their necks when they fight.

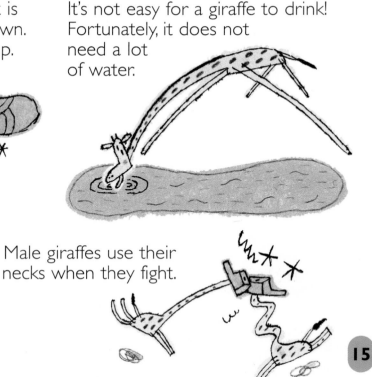

Alone and in groups

Giraffes usually live alone, but when danger threatens they group together to defend themselves.

Because of their long necks they can see danger from a long way off.

Each giraffe keeps watch over a different bit of the savannah.
The biggest giraffes protect the others.

Giraffes can recognise the members of their own group because each one has different markings.

The zebra

Zebras live in large groups to help protect themselves against their enemy – lions.

Zebras have stripes everywhere, even on their manes!

Every zebra has a different pattern of stripes.

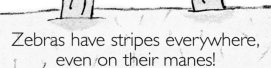

At the first sign of danger, zebras run away. They can run very fast for a long time.

19

The rhinoceros

The rhinoceros lives on its own.
It feeds on the thorny
shrubs that grow
in the savannah.

Birds live on its back: big ones
and small ones. They pick off
insects and warn of any danger.

When two rhinoceroses meet, they attack each
other with their horns, grunting loudly.

A rhinoceros
sweats a lot
and needs to
drink a lot.

Its main enemy is the mosquito.
It covers itself in mud to
keep the insects away.

Two horns – one big, one small

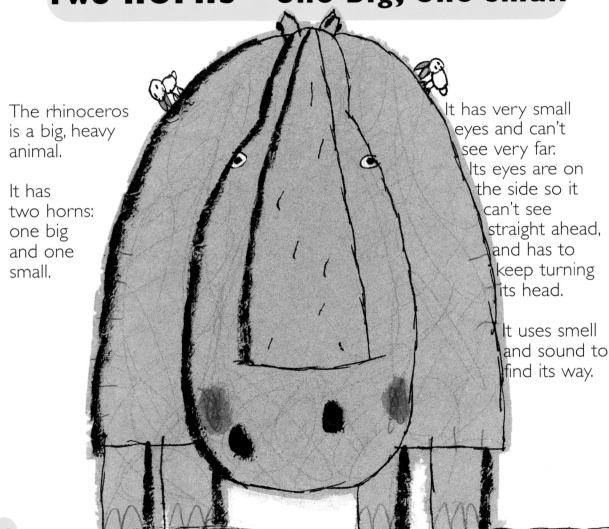

The rhinoceros is a big, heavy animal.

It has two horns: one big and one small.

It has very small eyes and can't see very far. Its eyes are on the side so it can't see straight ahead, and has to keep turning its head.

It uses smell and sound to find its way.

22

When it is born, a baby rhinoceros is very small. It has no horns.

Its mother protects her baby fiercely because without horns it can't defend itself.

Soon there may be no rhinos left, except in zoos, because they are hunted and killed by poachers, who sell their horns.

The **hippopotamus**

The hippopotamus spends its days in the water
to keep cool when the sun is hot.

In the evenings hippos all leave the water to go and graze.
They always follow the same paths.

Hippos eat at
night because they
don't like the sun.

Hippos big and small

A hippo has a big head and a huge mouth that opens very wide when it yawns.

Adult hippos look like a big barrel on four little feet!

When a hippo leaves the water, an oily red liquid comes out of its pores, which protects it from the sun.

Baby hippos learn to swim
before they can walk.
They suckle their mothers
under water without breathing,
then climb on her back to rest.

Until they are about two
years old, young hippos walk beside their
mothers, and the others follow behind in
single file, from the youngest to the oldest.

The Lion

In the evenings, at sunset, the king of the savannah opens his enormous mouth and lets out a great roar.

28

Lions don't like the heat.
They spend long days
sleeping in the shade
of a tree.

29

A king's life

Lions and lionesses are very different.
The lioness is smaller and more muscular.

The lion has an impressive mane
and whiskers around his mouth.

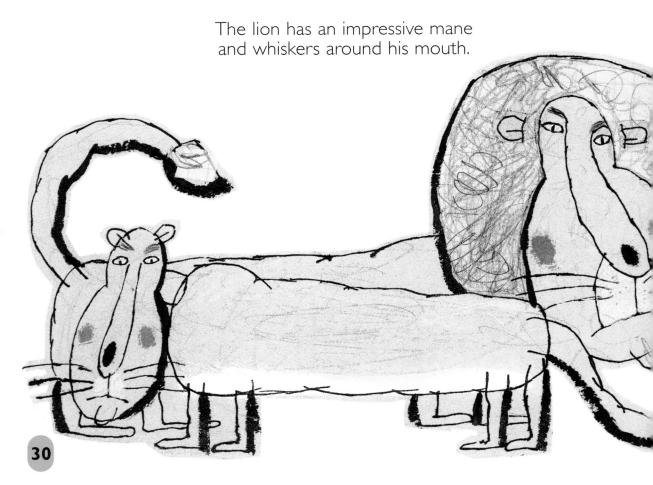

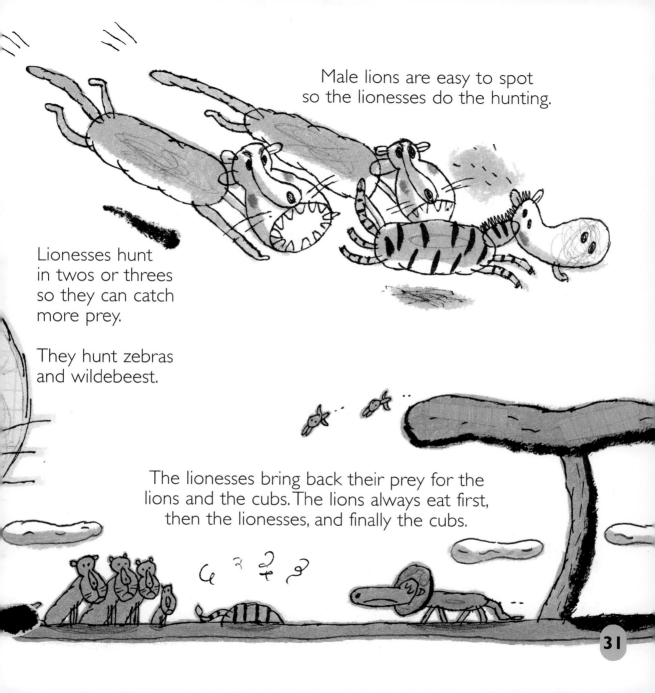

Male lions are easy to spot
so the lionesses do the hunting.

Lionesses hunt
in twos or threes
so they can catch
more prey.

They hunt zebras
and wildebeest.

The lionesses bring back their prey for the
lions and the cubs. The lions always eat first,
then the lionesses, and finally the cubs.

The cheetah

The cheetah is the fastest animal on Earth – it can run at up to 90 km/h. It belongs to the big-cat family, like lions and leopards.

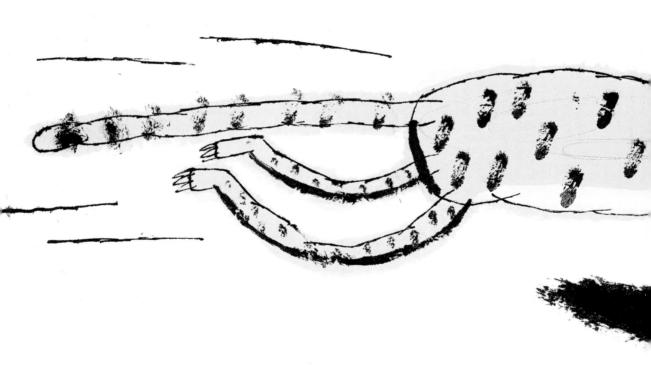

Cheetahs have a small round head and round ears. They have big paws and a long tail. Their fur is covered in small black markings.

A big hunter

The cheetah does not hunt at the same time as the lionesses and the panthers. It also chooses smaller animals, like the gazelle.

The cheetah can run very fast, but not for very long – it has to stop after about a minute and many of its prey escape.

The cheetah only likes fresh meat and eats its catch straight away.

At a year and a half, cheetahs are fully grown and can live alone.

Baby cheetahs are very small and vulnerable. Many of them are caught by eagles and hyenas. To protect them, their mothers change their hiding place every day.

Records

The **biggest** and the **greediest**

8 TONNES
6 TONNES
350 KG
110 KG

The **tallest**

The **oldest**

The **fastest**

Index

acacia tree 14
Africa 6
big-cat family 32
birds 10, 20
babies 13, 23, 27, 31, 35
breathing 11
cheetahs 32-35
   babies 35
   characteristics 33
   hunting 34, 35
   speed 32
climate 6
danger 16, 20
eagles 35
ears 33
elephants 8-13
   babies 13
   eating and drinking 9
   families 12
   female 12
   growth 9
   life expectancy 9
   male 11, 13
   size 9
   skin 10
   trunk 11
   weight 9
enemies 18, 21
evening 25, 28
eyes 22
fighting 15, 21
food and feeding 6, 9, 14, 15, 20,
   21, 25, 31
gazelles 34
giraffes 14-17
   eating and drinking 14, 15
   fighting 15
   groups 16, 17

male 15
markings 17
neck 14, 15, 17
sleeping 15
walking 15
grazing 25
habits 24, 25, 27
heads 26, 33
herds and groups 12, 13, 16, 17
hippopotamuses 24-27
   babies 27
   eating and drinking 25
   habits 24, 25, 27
   protection from the sun 26
   size 26
   swimming 27
horns 21, 22, 23
hunting 31, 34
hyenas 35
insects 10, 20, 21
leaves 9, 11, 14
leopards 32
lionesses 30, 31, 34
lions 18, 28-31, 32
   cubs 31
   eating and drinking 31
   habits 29
   mane 30
   size 30
   sleeping 29
markings 17, 18, 33
mosquitoes 21
mouths 26
mud 21
noises 11, 21, 28
panthers 34
paws 33
playing 13

poachers 23
prey 34, 35
protection 17, 18, 19, 23, 26, 35
rhinoceroses 20-23
   babies 23
   eating and drinking 20, 21
   enemies 21
   endangered 23
   eyes 22
   fighting 21
   horns 21, 22, 23
   weight 22
safari 7
savannah 6, 7, 17, 20, 30
size of safari animals 9, 14, 22, 26,
   36
skin 10
sleeping 13, 15, 29
smell 22
speed 19, 32, 34, 37
suckling 13, 27
sun 24, 25, 26
swimming 27
tails 33
tongues 14
trees 14, 29
trunk, uses 11
walking 15, 25, 27
water 11, 15, 24, 25, 26
weights of safari animals 9, 22
wildebeest 31
zebras 18-19, 31
   enemies 18
   manes 18
   markings 18
   speed 19
   zoos 23